i love card making

25 PROJECTS THAT WILL SHOW YOU HOW TO MAKE CARDS EASILY AND QUICKLY

AMY GOODA

PHOTOGRAPHY BY CHARLIE RICHARDS

KYLE CATHIE LTD

First published in Great Britain in 2007 by
Kyle Cathie Limited
122 Arlington Road
London NW1 7HP
general.enquiries@kyle-cathie.com
www.kylecathie.com

ISBN: 978-1-85626-743-4

Project editor: Jennifer Wheatley
Series design: Jenny Semple
Designer: Shelley Doyle
Photographer: Charlie Richards
Stylist: Vicki Murrell
Copy editor: Libby Willis
Production: Sha Huxtable and Alice Holloway
Models: Lise Manavit, Rachael Mossom, Avril Murphy, Heather Pennell, Roberta Pitrè, Tom Richards

A Cataloguing In Publication record for this title is available from the British Library.

Colour reproduction by Sang Choy
Printed in Singapore

i love card making

contents

my card-making story

At one point or another, everyone has made a handmade card, though for many the first and last time was probably when they were a small child. You may still think that the only person who would appreciate your creativity is your mum, but in fact everyone values the time and effort put into making a personalised card. People forget how easy and fun it is to make something, and even if you think you aren't very creative there are always ways to make a card that don't require you to be a Picasso. Card making is such an easy way to express your creative side and I think you'd be surprised by just how many different kinds of cards you can make.

I have made cards throughout my life and it remains the one hobby I always come back to. There are so many exciting papers and materials that something will always inspire me afresh. Even when I don't plan to make a card, I can't pass a craft shop

without going in. There is so much to tempt me that I never leave empty-handed! I always carry my notebook, too, because you never know when that brilliant idea will come!

Card making is a great way of making something out of nothing, and there are a million things you can do with leftover wrapping paper, magazines and fabric remnants. The market for craft products is so large that you can quite easily buy all your materials from the comfort of your home, using online stores or auction sites where you can find the best bargains. Use everything and anything as inspiration, from your favourite cushion cover to a treasured photograph. Most of all, have fun and enjoy the creative process!

Amy
X

Card Sizes

Embellishments

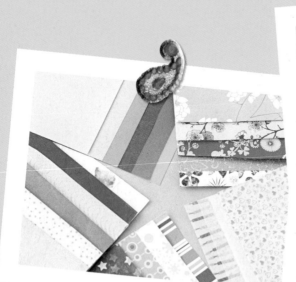

Paper and Card

Envelopes

Embossing

how to make cards

From basics such as cutting tools to more specialised equipment, this chapter will introduce you to everything you need to start card making. Just add your imagination and you'll be well on your way to creating fantastic designs!

paper and card

One of the main decisions in card making is choosing the right type of card for your project. There is a vast assortment of cards and papers out there, but this is a list of the main types.

Card stock is the basis for most handmade cards and comes in varying weights (thicknesses). Ideally, it is best to feel the card before you purchase it so you can decide if it is going to be heavy enough for your project. A few things to consider are whether the card will fold well (some cards are too thick to give a sharp crease) and if the card is thick enough to stand when folded. It also gives the card a feeling of good quality if it is a bit weighty. Sometimes the card or paper itself will be your inspiration for the design.

1 Coloured card: Even basic card comes in different forms, with many having different textured surfaces (linen, ribbed and hammered are examples), and the finish of the final card is something to consider when making your choice.

2 Handmade papers: Lightweight cards or papers are ideal for decorating the front of your card or folding to form an insert. There is a fabulous selection of handmade and natural papers in craft and art shops. These work well to embellish the card but can be glued to a thicker piece of card to create a card base. Mulberry card is a favourite among crafters – it is a lightweight handmade-effect paper that can be torn to create feathery, ripped edges.

3 Printed: Printed papers such as wrapping paper and scrapbook paper are widely available and are perfect for making cards. Scrapbook papers are lightweight and usually quite colourful, with a pattern or repeated image. Some are also printed with text that could be used on your cards. Preprinted designs can be used as a card base or for a background, or pieces of the design can be cut out and layered to create a 3D effect. It's also worth considering printing out your own designs from a computer, whether using Clipart or a scanned image or photo. Creating your own printed images means your designs will always be unique.

4 Vellum: This is another paper with many uses. Similar in feel and appearance to tracing paper, it is lightweight and semi-transparent. Use it for inserts or layered over different background colours. Decorated vellum is available with greetings and repeat patterns printed on. These work well mounted on coloured card or into an aperture.

5 Scraps: Keep leftover papers from Christmas and birthdays and gather interesting papers and materials from around the house so you have a range of materials to complement and contrast with those you buy. Paper bags, metal food trays and corrugated paper from chocolate boxes all have the potential to be reinvented. It's a good idea to keep the scraps and other bits left over when making your projects, as they could be reused in another design.

card sizes

Most of the cards I have created here have been made from an A4 (297 x 210mm) sheet of card. Whatever card base you wish to make, I recommend that you find the envelope to fit before you make it. That way you can make the card to fit the envelope – otherwise you will need to make your envelope (see page 32).

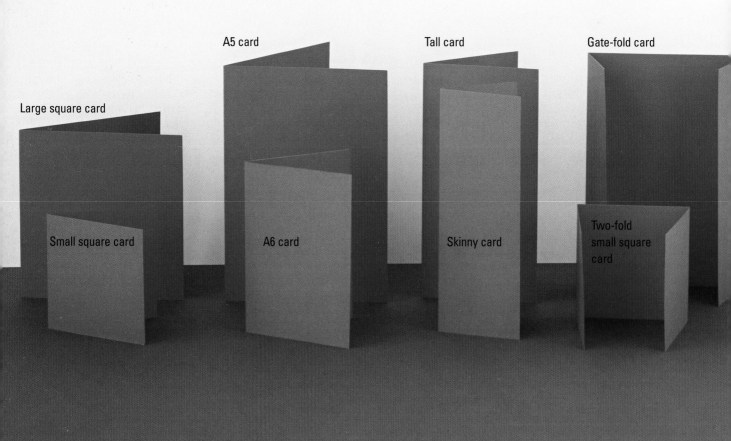

Large square card

A5 card

Tall card

Gate-fold card

Small square card

A6 card

Skinny card

Two-fold small square card

The sizes of the cards I have used are listed below along with the measurements for the available envelopes.

Be aware that if the card you are making has a raised element on the front, you may need to use a larger envelope to accommodate the design. Boxes are also available in a range of sizes designed to fit cards, so if your card is delicate or too bulky to go in an ordinary envelope, protect your hard work by using a box. They usually come flat-packed and many are suitable for posting.

Name of card base	Unfolded card size	Folded card base size (H x W)	Envelope size
Large square card	150 x 297mm	150 x 148.5mm	155 x 155mm
Small square card	100 x 200mm	100 x 100mm	105 x 105mm
A5 card	210 x 297mm (A4)	210 x 148.5mm	229 x 162mm
A6 card	148.5 x 210mm (A5)	148.5 x 105mm	162 x 114mm
Tall card	210 x 210mm	210 x 105mm	229 x 114mm
Skinny card	210 x 148.5mm (A5)	210 x 74mm	214 x 80mm
Gate-fold card	210 x 297mm (A4)	210 x 148.5mm (flaps are 74mm wide)	162 x 229mm
Two-fold small square card	100 x 297mm	100 x 99mm (flaps are 99mm wide)	105 x 105mm

cutting tools

You don't need to invest in any major equipment to create cards. If you're just starting out, a good craft knife and ruler can take the place of a paper trimmer and scoring tool.

1 Craft knife and ruler: Use a knife you feel comfortable with and keep your fingers beyond the cutting edge of the knife. I use a scalpel, which is lightweight and easy to control because of the small blade. Most craft knives are fairly small and have a retractable blade that can help prevent accidents. A raised ruler with a groove in the middle will also keep your fingers away from the edge. Although a plastic ruler is fine for measuring, ideally you should use a metal ruler to cut so you won't slice parts of the ruler or your fingers off with the knife. A ruler and craft knife can be used to measure and lightly score a card before folding. A rubber cutting mat is a wise buy to avoid scoring your desk or table.

2 Paper trimmer: A paper trimmer is an invaluable tool and a quick and easy way to achieve straight cut edges, saving you time and effort. There are many to choose from and they vary in size, quality and price. If you are planning to make a lot of cards, it is probably worth investing in a proper craft trimmer. It will come in useful for the following reasons:
1. You can use it to cut and score your card templates, lining the card up against the straight edge.
2. It has measurements on it and template outlines of some of the most popular paper sizes.
3. Some of the more expensive trimmers have changeable blades so you can create different edges on your cards such as deckle or perforations.

4. It is very handy when you're creating cards in bulk, for a wedding or Christmas, for example.

3 Circular cutters: There are a variety of cutters available that enable you to cut not only circular apertures but also ovals, hearts and other shapes when used with a stencil. These are specifically designed for the crafter and allow you to place an aperture exactly where you want (or simply cut a loose shape) without having the difficulty of cutting a curved edge by hand. I use a compass cutter in some of the projects here (it is like a set of compasses but with a blade instead of a pencil). It is a cheaper alternative but can be more difficult to use and will only cut circles.

4 Scissors: A good pair of quality scissors will always be an invaluable piece of equipment for any crafter. Have a small, sharp pointed pair for cutting out intricate patterns as well as ribbons, threads and handmade papers. Keep an old pair for cutting wires (or wire cutters if you prefer) and sticky tape so you don't ruin your good ones. I also keep a large, heavy pair of scissors that I only use on fabric to give a good finish but these are unnecessary unless you plan to use a lot of material. You can also buy scissors aith a decorative edge in a variety of different patterns which will create a fancy edge when used on paper or card.

adhesives

There is a vast range of glues available today and everyone has their special preference. Always read the manufacturer's guidelines on the packaging.

1 Double-sided tape: This is a clear tape that is sticky on both sides. It has numerous uses and is a very neat and secure way of attaching items to card. It is a good substitute for glue.

2 Masking tape: Masking tape can be used for lots of different things and is always handy to have. It is great for masking areas you want to leave uncovered or for temporarily attaching things to paper or card, as it is not sticky enough to rip the surface off.

3 Spray adhesive: This comes in a can and is ideal for using on large areas of paper or material, as well as very fine or transparent papers such as vellum or mulberry paper that require even coverage all over. It is very sticky so it is advisable to protect the area where you are working with scrap paper. Ideally, use this glue outside as you need to be in a well-ventilated area. With spray adhesive it is easy to reposition your work without the need to reapply the glue. It can be expensive but it gives a good finish, though you could substitute a glue stick for smaller work.

4 PVA craft glue: If you prefer to use a non-toxic glue, PVA will work in most cases, though it isn't strong enough to hold metal. Use a spreader for more intricate areas that require more precision. This glue dries clear but has a shine to it.

5 Glue gun: Glue guns are extremely useful for crafting as the glue is strong enough to hold heavy-weight materials. Glue guns heat up and melt glue sticks into hot glue that gives a strong hold. Glue sticks are usually clear but can be bought in a range of colours as well as glitter. The glue dries very quickly and there is less time to rearrange your design but it can hold wirework and heavier items on card. It can also be used to raise card and paper up from the background. Any mistakes can easily be picked off, whereas other glues can leave a shiny trail behind. Remember that glue guns and the glue in them are hot, so make sure you protect the surface underneath to stop the glue getting on your furniture!

6 3D foam squares: These are used for raising sections of work so you can introduce different levels to your design. They come in different sizes and are sticky on the top and bottom.

7 Multi-purpose craft glue: There are many different makes of household glue suitable for a range of uses. I find that general multi-purpose glue is a good all-rounder as it sticks light- and heavyweight card, material and metal. It also doesn't dry too rapidly, so you have the freedom to reposition things without rushing. It dries clear with a shine.

8 Glue stick: A glue stick is great for lightweight or sheer papers or materials where other glues would soak through. It remains hidden and is ideal if you want a very flat surface – just remember to smooth out any lumps. Again, you will be able to reposition most work when using a glue stick. Always replace the cap as the glue can dry out quickly.

cutting and scoring

HOW TO CUT AND SCORE

To cut a piece of card to size, you can use a paper trimmer or just a knife and ruler.

1 Simply score the card using a scoring tool or craft knife, either using the edge of your paper trimmer (lining it up with the measurements) or a ruler to create your straight line. Templates and scoring boards are available that give grooves for scoring a range of different sizes; you will need to use a scoring tool with these.

2 When you have scored the card, fold it down the line and use your fingers to line the edges up. The card is quite pliable so you can push it around if your measuring isn't quite accurate. Use your thumb or finger to sharpen the crease by pressing along the edge. If you prefer, use a bone folder or ruler to run down the crease to sharpen it up. Work on a flat surface as this will help keep the edges of the card crisp.

AMY'S TIP

A scoring tool has a point on each end with a tiny ball (these come in varying sizes) so the tool is smooth to use. These can also be used to emboss with. Bone folders are special scoring tools that can also be used to score card and make a sharp crease.

CUTTING AN INSERT

Inserts are very useful as they add weight to the card, giving it a feeling of quality and a professional finish. If you are making cards in bulk such as invitations for a special occasion, using preprinted inserts saves you time and the repetition of writing them out.

Inserts also add a personal touch and, provided the edges are straight (or equally cut if you're using decorative scissors) and the insert is centrally placed, they will look great. Personally, I tend to cut inserts so they are only a few millimetres smaller than the card they are going in so there is hardly any border. But this varies from card to card and there is no right or wrong way – it is entirely up to you.

① Open the card and use the right-hand side as your guide for placement (don't worry about lining up the insert up with the left-hand side of the card, unless the design requires it. The text inside a card is almost always on the right so the eye is drawn to this side). Fold the insert in half and open out again.

Using the top, bottom and right-hand edge to help you measure, place your folded insert so the edges are all equally spaced.

② Glue in place, with a light glue such as a glue stick, spray mount or glue dots, by adding glue down the middle edge only.

If you're using a transparent insert such as vellum, use invisible glue dots or secure in place by tying cord or ribbon round the card. Single-sheet inserts glued straight down on to the card look just as good, too, and work well for cards that open in the middle (like a gate-fold card).

cutting an aperture

An aperture is a 'window' in the card that you can use in all kinds of different ways. You can dangle objects such as beads or sequins in them or if you're feeling more adventurous you could use them to trap confetti between layers or reveal images inside the card. They can be a bit tricky to cut but practice makes perfect! Some of the cards in this book will have windows cut in them but feel free to either adapt the design or use a precut card base.

CUTTING A SQUARE APERTURE

Most cards have only one fold in them, which is quite straightforward to measure and score. These can open from side to side or from bottom to top. Other cards have to be scored twice to make three sections to the card. This is simply a case of careful measuring and scoring in the right place. Folding the card into three creates an extra flap to fold behind the front of the card. This enables you to mount things into the window and hides the construction. Remember that in this case the middle section of card will become the front.

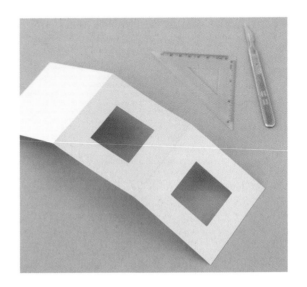

To cut an aperture, measure out where you want it to go by using a set square and pencil. This will ensure you have straight edges. Then simply cut out the aperture with your knife and a ruler.

CUTTING A CIRCULAR APERTURE

① To create a circular aperture, I find it easiest to cut a circle in the size I want in scrap paper. Then place it on the card front to see where it should be positioned. When you're happy with where it is, draw round it.

② Use a compass cutter to go over the line you have drawn. (Remember to work with your card base unfolded so you don't cut through the back of the card!).

AMY'S TIP

When cutting apertures or placing items on the front of the card, it works better visually to have slightly more space below than above. You may find this balances your design, particularly if you want to put a greeting below.

rubber stamps and punches

These days there is a huge variety of rubber stamps and punches available, covering every topic you could ever think of.

Rubber stamps are available through craft shops, online stores and even shopping channels. These include traditional wood-backed stamps and the more contemporary clear blocks with self-adhesive designs. The latter are great if you have difficulty positioning your stamps, as you can see exactly where the image will go. There are also companies that will make up personalised stamps to order. This is a good idea if you want your own design on a stamp or you need something specific for making a lot of cards such as wedding invitations.

There is also a wide range of inkpads for stamps that will give all kinds of effects. Some give a distressed, aged look whereas others can be used to stamp on glossy surfaces like acetate. Most inkpads will have a description of how the results will look or whether they are suitable for use on a glossy surface. Start with a basic coloured pad, then explore the market to see the range available and how you could develop your techniques.

❶ Make sure your stamp is clean. Press it on the inkpad, ensuring you have an even coverage.

AMY'S TIP

It is a good idea to test your inkpad and stamp beforehand on a scrap of the card you are using to see how much ink and pressure you need to apply.

② Position the stamp on your card and press down firmly, making sure you don't move it.

③ Leave to dry unless you wish to heat-emboss the image.

PUNCHES

There is such a variety of punches available that no sane card maker would be without at least one! Punches come in a range of different sizes and give all sorts of inspiring shapes you can think of. They are so useful for adding that personal touch to a design, as you can choose exactly what pattern to create. Every craft shop stocks them and most now come with a small lever for foolproof punching.

embossing

The embossing board is a fantastic piece of equipment that is so easy to use but gives instant results.

Follow the manufacturer's instructions and you can emboss designs on to a variety of materials including card, paper, vellum and sheet metal. Results vary depending on the materials, so practise first until you get the positioning right and remember to work on the reverse side. You can find stencils with all sorts of different patterns and borders.

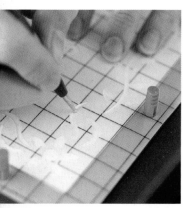

❶ Using the grid marked on the top of the stencil, line up your card or paper between the two layers of the stencil. Pressing firmly, use the small end of the embossing tool to draw round the outline of the stencil. Use the larger end to fill in any space, as you would if you were colouring in.

❷ Once you have completed the design, remove your card from the embossing board and turn over to reveal the image.

Sheet metal looks great when embossed and has a really professional finish. Use it with the embossing board or create your own freehand design. Simply draw your image on to the metal with a felt-tip pen and, using your scoring tool or embossing stylus, trace over the image, pressing firmly. As long as you do this on a firm but soft surface (like foam), you will get an embossed image. I've found that my best results come from using carpet as a backing. It gives perfect results every time!

Small hand-held embossers are also available. These look like punches and are quick and easy to use. Some of these fit on to corners and are extremely useful for adding that finishing touch.

METAL

Metal is so pliable that it extends itself to a lot of different techniques. Although it can be expensive to buy, it is well worth trying and even just using a small piece can really make a design work. It comes in silver, gold and copper colour and is soft enough to cut with a pair of scissors. Use it with embossers, free-hand embossing or punches, or simply cut out shapes by hand.

AMY'S TIP

If you want to try the metal sheeting but feel it costs too much, a metal tray from a takeaway or jam tart will give the same results. Remember to wash them clean first though!

heat-embossing

Heat-embossing is a completely different technique from normal embossing (described on the previous pages). Heat-embossing creates a slightly raised effect on your stamped design and can give a really professional touch to your image.

To heat-emboss you will need a rubber stamp, an inkpad, embossing powder and a heat tool. A heat tool is used to heat the embossing powder until it melts. The heat tool does not blow hot air like a hairdryer so don't use it instead!

You can achieve all sorts of effects through heat embossing using different powders or inkpads. Embossing powder is a fine powder that is tipped over a stamped image. It comes in a wide range of colours, including metallic and glitter-effect, and mixing powders together will give a unique appearance. Experiment by printing an image in one colour and then using a different-coloured embossing powder on top. Different combinations will change the end result.

You can create various effects when you emboss rubber-stamped images, especially if you choose to colour in your design. Flock powder is also available; this works in a similar way to embossing powder but gives a finish that feels like flock wallpaper.

I have used basic techniques in the projects but there is scope for you to develop your own variations on techniques. I like the embossing pens that work in the same way as a pad of ink. Simply draw your own image, cover it with embossing powder and heat. This is ideal for those who don't like rubber stamping or want to embellish a card in their own way.

1 Stamp your image with your chosen colour.

2 Before it has time to dry, cover the image with embossing powder.

3 Tip the excess off the image (the powder can be poured back in the jar to use again, so make sure you have scrap paper to hand to catch it all).

4 Hold the heat tool about 10cm away from the image and heat it until the powder starts to melt. Don't overheat it – a small area takes only a few seconds. Remember to do this on a protected or heatproof surface.

other techniques

Here are some other techniques to consider as part of your card-making repertoire! See the Gallery section for even more ideas.

EYELETS AND BRADS

Eyelets are designed specifically for card- and scrapbook-making and are available in a variety of shapes, colours and sizes. Simply use an eyelet tool to make a hole, add your front and back eyelet and use the eyelet tool to hammer it closed. (Always follow the manufacturer's guidelines.) Eyelets are great for attaching things to a card, holding something in place or tying ribbon or cord through. Brads are similar but easier to use, as no hammering is required. Brads come in the same vast range as eyelets and are like miniature paper fasteners. Make your hole, with a knife or an eyelet tool, push the legs of the brad through and open on the other side to secure. Again, these can simply hold papers in place or can be highlighted as the central feature of the design.

SEWING

Machine sewing has lots of uses and gives a nice touch to a card. It's a technique that is being used more and more in commercial cards nowadays. Using a sewing machine speeds things up but if you don't own one or prefer not to use a machine, then handsewing will give a

good result, too. Keep in mind a sewing machine's capabilities and don't push it too far. Use light papers and cards and check you have the right needle for the job. You have limited space under the machine foot, so pick a card size that will fit in the space and plan your design before you start. Stitching is an interesting way to attach layers to each other. Experiment with different stitches to create your own backgrounds and see the results you get when you punch holes without any thread.

LETTERING

Text can be a major part of a card design and play an important part in conveying your message to the recipient. Working wording into your design is simple and there are many ways to do it.

A computer is perfect for adding greetings to your card bases – be adventurous and add words in all directions. Have text running up the edge of the card or use it as a border. Of course, you aren't limited to computers; use text from stamps and stickers as well as transfers to say exactly what you want. Be inventive – there are countless ways to add wording so it becomes a feature of the design rather than an add-on. For example, tie your greeting on with ribbon like a luggage label or form the image itself out of decorative text.

If you prefer the hand-finished touch, writing your greeting in freehand can work equally well. When adding any text, first remember to measure, or mark in pencil, where you want to put it.

Font tips

* Decorative fonts like Lucida are good for occasions like weddings and anniversaries

* Sans serif fonts like Helvetica and Arial look clean and modern

* Serif fonts like Palatino and Georgia are good for when you want a more traditional look

* Handwritten fonts like Chalkboard strike an informal note

embellishments

Most embellishments speak for themselves. Here are just a few but feel free to think of lots of others and of fun ways to use them!

① **Beads, buttons and confetti:** Beads add a delicacy to designs and can be sewn on or threaded on to wire. Use jewellery-making beads or cheaper card-making beads that also come in a range of shapes. Buttons give a nice touch to a card and they come in such a variety that you can find ones suitable for every occasion. Craft shops sell buttons designed for card making but you will also find a range available in your local haberdashery. Confetti comes in an array of shapes, sizes and colours. It can be glued on to your design, trapped between layers or added loose inside the card as a surprise when opened!

② **Stickers:** Peel-off stickers have many uses in card making and there are untold numbers available. In a fantastic range of topics and colours, peel-offs can be added to a design or used as the main feature. Peel off an outline, mount on different coloured card from your card base and cut out, or use felt-tip pens specifically designed for colouring in stickers.

③ **Ribbons:** There are umpteen types and colours of ribbon to choose from. Why not layer different thicknesses on top of one another, wrap them around cards to hold inserts in place or close a card by tying it with ribbon, finishing with a bow?

④ **Wire:** Great used as an embellishment on its own, wire can be wrapped round something, glued on to a background, twisted or coiled like springs or threaded through beads. Wire comes in a range of colours and gauges (thicknesses) so you can pick exactly the right one for its intended use.

Other things to keep handy when you're crafting are a pencil, ruler, coloured pencils, felt-tip pens and metallic gel pens for adding detail to a design.

envelopes

Making your own envelopes is great fun and solves the problem of finding the right-sized envelope for a card. The perfect finishing touch!

Make envelopes as simple or as decorated as you like, incorporating the design on the card into the envelope. Alternatively, plain bought envelopes cry out to be decorated and it doesn't take much effort to customise them.

An envelope can be made from almost anything and it's worth experimenting with unusual materials for exciting results. Wrapping paper, card stock and handmade paper will all look great but more unusual materials such as vellum, plastic, fabric or even pages from a magazine can add a truly unique note. Even a simple piece of paper folded around a card and tied with yarn or string can create impact – it's also a handy option when you can't find your glue!

Envelopes are so easy to make that you won't want to stop at just one! Follow the steps below to produce an envelope from scratch but you could also simply unfold a bought envelope and use that as your template.

HOW TO MAKE YOUR OWN ENVELOPE

1 Lay your card base on your chosen piece of paper (it is advisable to use a larger piece than you think is necessary). Draw around the outline of the card with a pencil. Add at least an extra 10mm to the length and width (more if your card is bulky as it will need more paper to cover it), then draw this new outline in pencil. Now score down each of these outlines with the scoring tool.

2 Draw a flap for each edge of the envelope starting with the bottom flap, which will be the biggest. Make the width of this bottom flap large enough to cover about three-quarters of the size of the outlined section. Angle the edges slightly so they slope in from the centre. Draw a flap on either side approximately 20mm wide, again angling the edges slightly. This angle on the edges is important as it will help give a neater corner when the envelope is folded together. Repeat the process to draw the top flap that will cover the upper quarter of the outlined section. Add about 20mm to this as an overlap.

3 Cut out the envelope and fold the side sections in so they lie flat.

4 Add glue down the side edges of the bottom flap and secure over the side sections. Add more glue to secure if necessary. Make sure you are precise with the glue or you might stick the insides of the envelope together! Use a strip of double-sided tape or glue to secure the top flap in place once you have inserted your card.

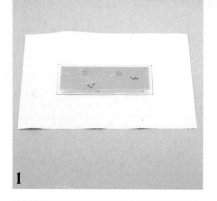

1

2

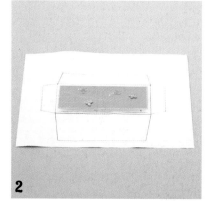

3

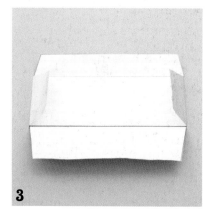

4

Child's Birthday

General Birthday

Girl's Birthday

Guy's Birthday

Present Card

birthday cards

The cards in this section cover a range of
birthday themes that are easily adapted
to suit just about everyone's special day.
Mix and match the ideas to send
the perfect message!

present card

This birthday card is ideal for men and women of all ages and is easily adapted for a variety of occasions. The unusual way of folding the card and the curved edge at the top add interest, creating something a bit different!

MATERIALS: White linen A5 card base (unfolded)
Extra white card
Turquoise decorative paper
Turquoise pearl A6 card
Silver cord

TOOLS: Craft knife, cutting mat, ruler
Embossing tool and board
Scissors
Masking tape
Craft glue

STEP 1
Create the card base using the white linen card. To do this, score and fold the card in half, then score a line down the centre of the front of the card. Fold this towards you so one side of the inside of the card is exposed.

STEP 2
Using the template below at your preferred size, trace the shape for the top of the card on to the card base. Carefully cut out the shape.

Edging template

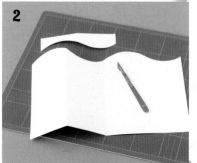

STEP 3

Using the embossing tool and board, emboss tiny stars and dots along the top and bottom of the card. Follow the shape you have cut at the top of the card. Draw a pencil line to follow on the underside of the card if you find this easier.

STEP 4

Using the present template below, cut out two large present shapes in white card, cover one with your decorative paper and trim. Cut out five small presents from the turquoise card.

STEP 5

Wrap the silver cord round the large turquoise present, using pieces of masking tape to secure at the back as you go. Glue the large white present shape to the back of this present. Tie a small bow from the silver cord and glue into position. Wrap each small present with cord and add a bow, securing with masking tape at the back.

Turn the large present over so you are working on the reverse, and apply glue down the right-hand side of the back only. Position it on the card so only half the present is stuck down and the other half remains unattached. Position the small presents along the card and glue into place. They will be slightly raised because of the cord and masking tape on the back.

Present template

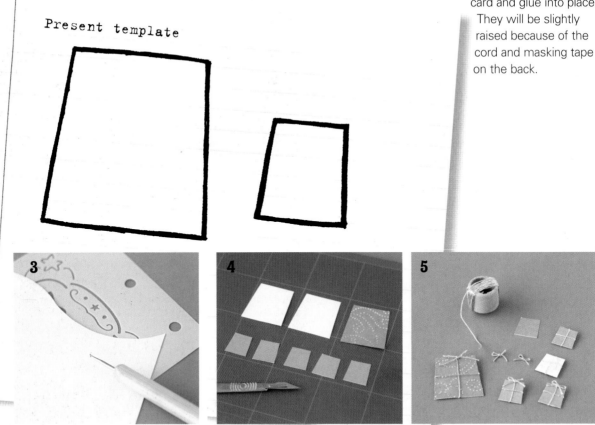

VARIATION

Variations on this theme are so easy to make and by using the same principles you could come up with any number of designs! If you want to make the card a bit more grown-up (for an 18th or 21st for example), why not try making the numbers smaller and trap them behind an acetate-covered aperture. Add glitter and small confetti before you seal it and decorate the rest of the card using small numbers or punched-out shapes.

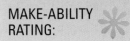
child's birthday

Using the number as the design can come in handy when you're struggling for ideas. Choose your own font to create the perfect design for the recipient whether they're young or just young at heart!

MATERIALS:
Turquoise large square card base
Sheet of turquoise scrapbook paper with a birthday design
Gold card
3D foam squares
Gold cord

TOOLS:
Craft knife, ruler, cutting mat
Scissors
Craft glue

STEP 1

Make a template of your chosen number and draw round it on to the scrapbook paper. Remember to have the template the wrong way round if you are working on the reverse of the paper. Cut this out so it has straight edges. Use the template to create a larger number in the gold card and mount the scrapbook number on to it. Turn over and add 3D foam squares to the back.

STEP 2

Use the remainder of the scrapbook paper to cut out two balloons. If your paper doesn't have balloons in the pattern, simply cut out balloon shapes in two colours similar to those in the scrapbook paper.

STEP 3

Secure the number on to the centre of the card front and glue the balloons in the top right corner so they overlap slightly. Cut two lengths of gold cord and glue these under the ends of the balloons so they hang down. Arrange the trailing cord so it is tucked behind the number.

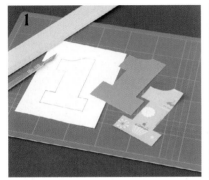
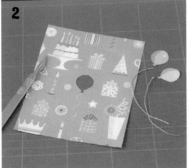
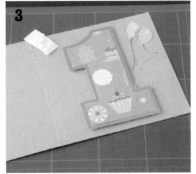

girl's birthday

This is a really quick card with a lovely feminine touch. It also has a strong contemporary feel and could be used for any number of occasions.

MATERIALS: Brown A6 card base
Turquoise card (148 x 105mm)
Brown card (148 x 105mm)
A range of scrap pearl card in various colours
2 x 4mm clear gems

TOOLS: Craft knife, ruler, cutting mat
Craft glue
Small and medium daisy punch
Medium dragonfly punch

STEP 1

Using the brown card base as a guide, trim the turquoise card so it is smaller than the front of the card to create a border. Do the same with the brown card, trimming it smaller than the turquoise card. Glue the brown card centrally on the turquoise card.

STEP 2

Punch out large and small daisies in a variety of colours. Trim alternate petals off some to create a variation. Stick two small daisies on top of two larger daisies of a contrasting colour. Cut out two green leaf shapes to add to the daisies.

STEP 3

Arrange all the shapes along the bottom left corner of the card, spreading them upwards so they overlap. Fix the daisies into place with a dot of glue, lifting the petals away from the card to create a 3D effect. Glue the gems on to the centre of two of the daisies. Punch out a dragonfly and position it in the top area of the card. Glue the body down, lifting the wings away from the card. Finally, add 3D foam dots on the reverse of the card and secure in position on the front of the card base.

VARIATION

It isn't necessary to use a computer for this project as you can create the lines in a variety of different ways. Use felt-tip pens or coloured pencils to give a vibrant look to the brown card, be adventurous and try wrapping coloured ribbons round the card, or simply cut strips of paper and layer them on. This card would be great for a girl's birthday as well, making the stripes in varying shades of pinks. And make this design with different-coloured card bases to see where your experimenting takes you!

guy's birthday

It can be difficult to think of designs for men but the options for developing this idea are endless. Metal is great for adding that masculine touch and bold coloured stripes on brown bring a contemporary look to the theme.

MATERIALS: Brown A6 card base
Silver sheet metal
Red card
Brown card
3D foam squares

TOOLS: Computer and printer
Craft knife, ruler, cutting mat
Embossing tool and board
Star stencil
Multi-purpose glue

STEP 1

Use a computer to print lines in various colours and thicknesses on the front section of the brown card base. Cut a strip of metal about 65 x 25mm using the knife and ruler. Metal can be difficult to cut so use scissors if this proves easier. Cut a 67 x 27mm strip of red card and a 69 x 29mm strip of brown card (adjust the size of these if your metal strip has turned out a different size). They should form an equal-looking border when layered on top of one another.

STEP 2

Using the sheet of metal and the embossing tool and board, emboss a column of three stars down the metal.

STEP 3

Stick the metal on to the red strip, then on to the brown strip, making sure the border is even. Add 3D foam squares to the reverse and position this on the front of the card in the centre towards the top.

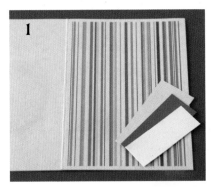

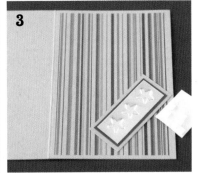

general birthday

This card is ideal to have as back-up when you don't have time to make one. It is suitable for both men and women and for a variety of occasions. Make a few so you have a supply for those card emergencies!

MATERIALS: Silver tall card base
Polypropylene sheet (medium weight)
Silver cord or elastic
Turquoise pearl paper
Purple pearl paper

TOOLS: Craft knife, ruler, cutting mat
Circular cutter
Craft glue

STEP 1

Cut the polypropylene to create a card base slightly larger than the silver card. Score down the middle, using a craft knife, to make a fold. Cut three different-sized holes randomly in the half of the plastic that will be the front, using the circular cutter.

STEP 2

Tie the silver card base and the polypropylene together with the cord or elastic, tying a knot at the top and trimming the ends, leaving some length. Cut circles out of the turquoise and purple papers, cutting smaller circles out of them to create rings. Make sure three of these circles are the same size as the holes you have cut out of the polypropylene, so they are revealed when the card is held shut. Cut a variety of other rings to fit inside the three main ones.

STEP 3

Holding the card and polypropylene shut, glue the main rings on to the silver card. Glue the remaining rings inside them. Use the leftover middles to decorate the edges of the card, cutting them in half first.

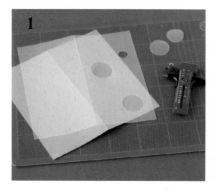
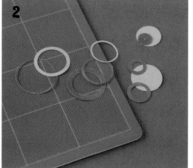
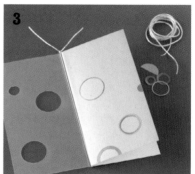

VARIATION
Polypropylene is an unusual material to use but gives the card the feeling of being professionally made. Experiment with this material on other designs, cutting different apertures or using it as a layer over your card. Why not try decorating it with brads or eyelets for a really eye-catching design?

Easter Bunnies

Candles

Festive Stars

Christmas Tree

Snowflakes

festive cards

With so many yearly celebrations, there is always an excuse to make a card. Use these festive designs to help you get started, and try a fresh approach such as spray paint or a basic pop-up card.

VARIATION

This is a good chance to work with bold colours if, like me, you tend to shy away from them. Why not use handmade or mulberry paper in an exotic pink or rich purple to mimic the texture and luxurious colours of Indian fabric. Add as many paisley embellishments as you like!

bollywood

This makes an incredibly glamorous birthday card but is also ideal for celebrating the Indian festival of Diwali. The design can be easily replicated to make large quantities for a stunning Indian-themed wedding invitation.

MATERIALS:
Green pearl A5 card base
Green pearl card
Gold card
1 x green paisley gem
4 x gold peel-off flower strips
4 x 3D foam squares

TOOLS:
Craft knife, ruler, cutting mat
Craft glue

STEP 1

From the extra green pearl card, cut out a square measuring 35 x 35mm. Then take the gold card and cut out two squares, one measuring 40 x 40mm and the other 30 x 30mm. Stick the squares on top of each other with the glue, alternating the colours (gold – green – gold). When the glue has dried, centre the paisley gem on top of the gold square and stick down.

STEP 2

Take the gold peel-off flower strips and cut four 140mm-long strips (that is, the width of the card). Place two along the bottom of the card and two along the top of it to create a border effect. It's a good idea to use the ruler at this point to ensure the lines are straight.

STEP 3

Finally, attach a 3D foam square to each corner on the back of the paisley square and position it so it is centred towards the top. Stick down.

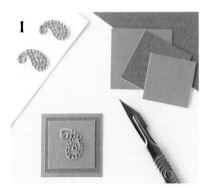

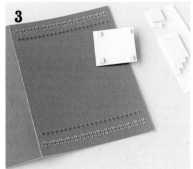

snowflakes

Using heat-embossing in this design really brings out the sparkle of the snowflakes.

MATERIALS: Blue pearl large square
card base
2 large silver snowflake confetti
3 x 320mm lengths of ribbon in
three different thicknesses
(blue satin, white organza and
white satin with silver edging)

TOOLS: Circular cutter
Snowflake stamp
Silver inkpad
Silver embossing powder
Embossing heat tool
Craft glue
Small white stickers

STEP 1

Cut a circle in the bottom right corner of the card base. Make sure it is large enough to fit the confetti inside.

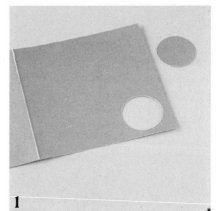

STEP 2

Cover your working area with scrap paper and keep the card base unfolded. Use the snowflake stamp and the silver ink to make a pattern on the front of the card. Add embossing powder, shake off the excess and fix in place with the heat tool.

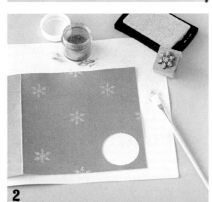

STEP 3

Glue the two snowflake confetti together (back to back), trapping a small piece of ribbon between them.

3

STEP 4

Layer the ribbons on top of each other according to their widths. Wrap them around the left-hand side of the card from top to bottom.

4

STEP 5

Overlap the ends of the ribbon inside the card and glue them into place. This will hide the glue and keep the card looking neat. Trim the ends to make sure they are straight. Attach the snowflake from the inside of the card so it hangs in the circular aperture. Secure it in place with a small white sticker.

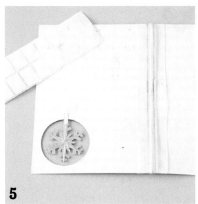

5

VARIATION

Don't worry if you don't want to use heat-embossing on this card or you're looking for a quicker alternative. Using festive wrapping paper with snowflakes on your card base and simply adding the confetti and ribbon will give great results, too. Alternatively, this card would also work well without the aperture – just apply the confetti to the surface of the card and add ribbon.

VARIATION
This card would work with any stamp of your choice providing you cut the aperture large enough. You could always add a little more festive sparkle by using embossing powder and a heat tool to lift the design. Use other bright festive colours for the card base and stamp such as red, gold and silver to really convey the feeling of Christmas.

christmas tree

Christmas cards don't need to be too elaborate to convey the season's greetings. Keeping the design simple often has more impact than going over the top.

MATERIALS: Green pearl small square card base
Small gold star confetti
Red dots

TOOLS: Compass cutter
Cutting mat
Small Christmas tree stamp
Green inkpad
Craft glue

STEP 1

Cut a circular aperture in the front of the card base measuring about 40mm across. It is a good idea to check how large your stamped image will be by practising on scrap paper; if it doesn't fit inside the aperture, enlarge the aperture. Remember to work with the card unfolded, or you'll cut through the back of the card as well.

STEP 2

Ink up your stamp, practise stamping the image a few times on scrap paper and then fold the card shut. Stamp the image through the aperture on to the inside of the card, positioning it in the centre of the aperture. Leave to dry.

STEP 3

Decorate the tree with a gold star and the red dots. Finish by gluing a row of stars along the top and bottom edges of the card.

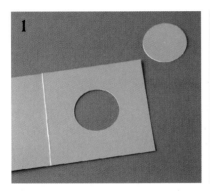

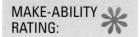
festive stars

Spray painting may not usually be associated with card making but you can achieve some really striking, instant results. It's great if you want to make a batch of cards for a celebration such as Christmas or Thanksgiving.

MATERIALS: Red pearl (double-sided) large
square card base
2 sizes of star ribbon (any colour)
2 sizes of star confetti (any colour)

TOOLS: Masking tape
Blue tack
Scrap paper/newspaper
Protective mask
Gold spray paint

STEP 1

Arrange the star ribbons down the left-hand side of the card so the two sizes slightly overlap. Secure the ribbons in place with folded masking tape. Try to stick down as many stars as possible as the air from the aerosol will lift the loose stars away from the card. Arrange loose star confetti randomly next to the ribbon and secure in place with blue tack.

STEP 2

When you're happy that the stars are all secure, cover your working area (even if you're working outside) with scrap paper/newspaper. Remember to cover the back of the card if you're working with it flat or the inside if you are working with it folded shut.

STEP 3

Wear a mask, then spray the card, leaving the right-hand side less heavily sprayed than the left. Leave it to dry in a well-ventilated area. Once it is dry, remove the stars from the card to reveal your image.

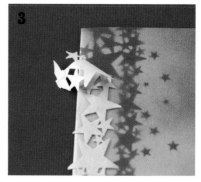

VARIATION

Red and gold are really festive colours so why not use them to create cards for other celebrations such as Chinese New Year. Or make this card even more suitable for Thanksgiving by using red, white and blue and masking areas to create stripes. If you prefer not to use spray paint, you could try using paint and a brush to splatter paint over the stencil. Or if you want to create your own image, simply use masking fluid to draw your own designs freehand, spray and then peel off.

candles

Pop-up cards don't have to be just for children. This simple but elegant festive card proves how decorating the card inside as well as out can really create a feature. It's lovely for Hannukah as well as birthdays.

MATERIALS: White linen A6 card base
Clear or white vellum/tracing
paper (210 x 297mm)
Yellow and orange
coloured pencils
Silver insert (162 x 114mm)
Silver sheet metal
Silver elastic

TOOLS: Digital camera
Candle
Computer and printer
Knife, ruler, cutting mat
Small scissors
Glue stick/invisible glue dots

STEP 1

Photograph a lit candle and use a computer to duplicate the image nine times. If you prefer not to use a computer, you could use scrapbook paper, transfers or simply draw candles yourself. Create two images from the candles: one with the candles in a pyramid formation and another with the candles in a row at various different heights. Print out these images on to the sheet of vellum. Add more colour to the flames, if needed, with the coloured pencils.

Cut out the pyramid formation of candles, following the sloping angles the candles form. Cut the bottom of the candles at 45° so these have sloping edges as well.

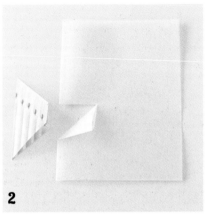

STEP 2

Create an insert from the vellum (this should be slightly smaller than the silver insert you are using). Keeping the insert folded shut, make a cut with the knife and ruler. Cut through both layers, starting from the fold; the cut should measure half the width of the candle pyramid cutout. When the insert is opened out this cut should be the same width as the cutout. Close the insert and fold the cut edge at 45°.

Fold the pyramid in half lengthways and crease.

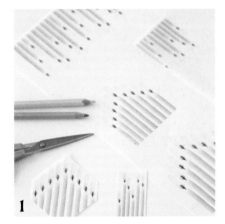

STEP 3

Push the V-shaped section you have just created through to the inside of the insert so it opens out as shown.

3

STEP 4

The candle pyramid printout should fit over this V-shaped section. Use a light glue to secure it, such as a glue stick or invisible glue dots.

4

STEP 5

Cut a section from the other candle photograph, approximately 25 x 45mm. Mount this on to a piece of silver sheet metal measuring 50 x 30mm (so it has a 5mm border). Secure together with a glue stick or invisible glue dots and use craft glue to attach the whole thing to the top centre of the front of the card.

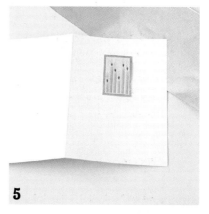

5

STEP 6

Layer the card base, silver insert and vellum insert on top of each other and tie together with the elastic, tying a knot at the bottom of the card, letting the ends hang down. You will need to make a small hole in the vellum at the point of the V for the elastic to pass through.

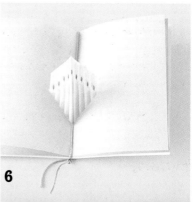

6

VARIATION

Pop-up cards really aren't complex to make. Once you have got the hang of it, you can use this base to experiment with different sizes and positions for any theme.

VARIATION

With so many Easter-themed craft materials around the options for adapting this design are many. Why not try a fluffy chick or an egg instead of a rabbit? Or adapt it for a different festive occasion such as Christmas using themed wrapping paper and a cutout of a snowman, penguin or Santa in the centre. Or why not cover the card with greengrocer's grass to give it that look of spring, adding punched-out daisies to complete the look!

easter bunnies

This is a bright, cheerful card that is a sweet way to let someone know you're thinking of them, and add a spring to their step!

MATERIALS:
White small square card base
Small piece of gingham wrapping paper
Yellow card or paper (95 x 95mm)
Easter paper with rabbits
Mini 3D foam squares
Gold Easter egg peel-off stickers
Patterned wrapping paper

TOOLS:
Spray mount
Craft knife, ruler, cutting mat
Set square
Scissors

STEP 1

Cut the yellow gingham wrapping paper to the same size as the card base, adding a few millimetres on the width to allow for the crease when the card is folded. Use spray mount to secure to the card, checking that the card can still fold easily. Cut an aperture in the front of the card measuring 45 x 45mm.

STEP 2

Glue the piece of yellow card inside the card on the right-hand side. Carefully cut out a rabbit from the Easter paper (if the paper is quite thin, you may want to back it with card before you cut it out). Add mini 3D foam squares all over the reverse of the rabbit (cut up large ones if you can't get mini ones) and position on the yellow background so he is in the middle of the aperture when the card is closed.

STEP 3

Stick a row of Easter egg stickers on to the patterned wrapping paper. Carefully cut around them with scissors. Cut them into lengths of three eggs and position round the sides of the aperture. Glue into place.

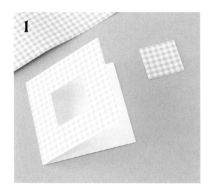

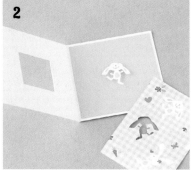

You're a Star!

Mother's Day

Get Well

New Home

New Baby

occasion cards

This section covers a selection of various
special occasions you might make a card
for. By using these ideas you can
develop your own designs covering
any occasion from a party
to simply saying
'hello'!

you're a star!

This card looks so intricate that the recipient will instantly appreciate how much effort you've put into it. It's actually very simple to do but will make a great impression and is just right for saying well done or congratulations, or for letting someone know how much you value them.

MATERIALS: White linen card (210 x 297mm)
Silver coloured wire (24-gauge)
Silver star beads
Silver long beads

TOOLS: Craft knife, ruler, cutting mat
Set square
Embossing tool and board
Double-sided tape
Craft glue

STEP 1

Cut the card base from the white card so it measures 100 x 280mm. Score and fold the base into three panels each measuring just under 100 x 100mm. Cut a square aperture in the centre and right-hand panels, measuring 45 x 45mm. When you fold the right-hand panel behind the centre the apertures should line up. The centre panel will be the front of the card.

STEP 2

Turn the card base over so you are working on the reverse. Emboss a row of tiny squares along the top and bottom of the centre panel, using the embossing board. Cut three pieces of wire 60mm

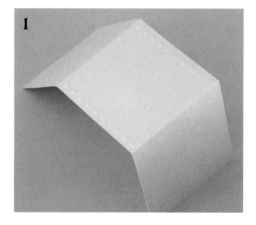

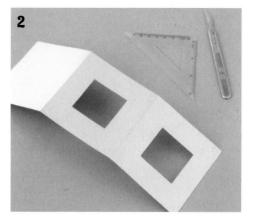

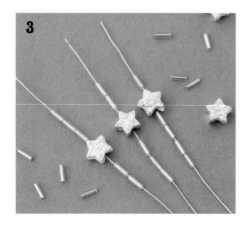

long to fit across the aperture. I have fitted five beads and one star within the aperture but if your beads are longer or shorter you may wish to adjust the aperture or use fewer beads.

STEP 3
Slide one long bead on to a piece of wire, followed by a star and then four more long beads. This will be your top row of beads. For the middle row, slide two beads on to a piece of wire, followed by a star and then three more beads. For the bottom row, add three beads, one star and then two more beads to the piece of wire.

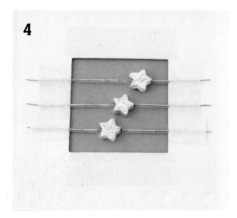

STEP 4
Place the middle row over the aperture from the reverse of the card. Once positioned, secure it in place with double-sided tape. Do the same with the top and bottom rows, straightening the wire if needed. Always place the middle row first as this will give you a good idea of where to place the other two rows so they are equally spaced.

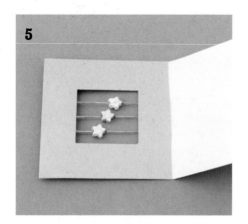

STEP 5
Trim the ends of the wire if they stick out. Peel off the tape backing and add more around the top and bottom of the aperture. Add glue around the edges of the centre panel of the card and then close the two apertures together, smoothing them shut.

valentine's day

There's nothing like creating a handmade card to show someone how much you love them. With minimum effort you can create this stylish Valentine's card for a guy or a girl.

MATERIALS: Black tall card base
Red tall card base
5mm red gems

TOOLS: Craft knife, ruler, cutting mat
Embossing tool and board
Craft glue

STEP 1
Trim the red card base so that when it is folded round the outside of the black card base the bottom, top and outside edges expose 10mm of the black card underneath as a border. Don't attach the card bases together yet.

STEP 2
Using the embossing board, emboss a row of hearts down the right-hand side of the red card. Emboss a larger heart centred towards the top of the card.

STEP 3
Glue the red outer card around the black card so the black card is visible. Finish by adding a red gem to the top right of each heart, including the large one.

VARIATION
To make a more masculine version, simply reverse the colours so the black card is in front. You could also add just one embossed heart in the centre or cut out a heart-shaped aperture to reveal the red inside the card.

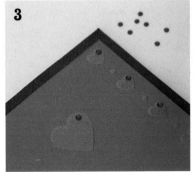

wedding invitation

This has to be one of the quickest and easiest designs in this book, which makes it ideal for producing in large quantities for a wedding. The image is very cost-effective without compromising the impact.

MATERIALS: White tall card base
20mm white organza ribbon
White scrap card
3 clear flower gems
Sheet of vellum with wedding design
(210 x 210mm)

TOOLS: Scissors
Small and large daisy punches
Craft glue
Glue stick

STEP 1
Wrap white organza ribbon round the left side of the front of the card. Tie the ribbon near the bottom front of the card, so that the card will stand up. Leave the lengths quite long but trim the ends at an angle to give a nice sharp finish.

STEP 2
Punch out one large and three small daisies from the white scrap card. Glue a small daisy on to the large daisy, then glue flower gems into the centre of the three small daisies. Glue the flowers to the card in a horizontal row towards the top of the card.

STEP 3
Cut the vellum down so it is slightly smaller than the card base and glue in to the card using a glue stick. (See page 19 for more on cutting and gluing inserts).

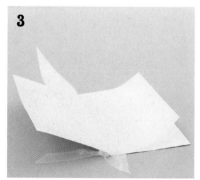

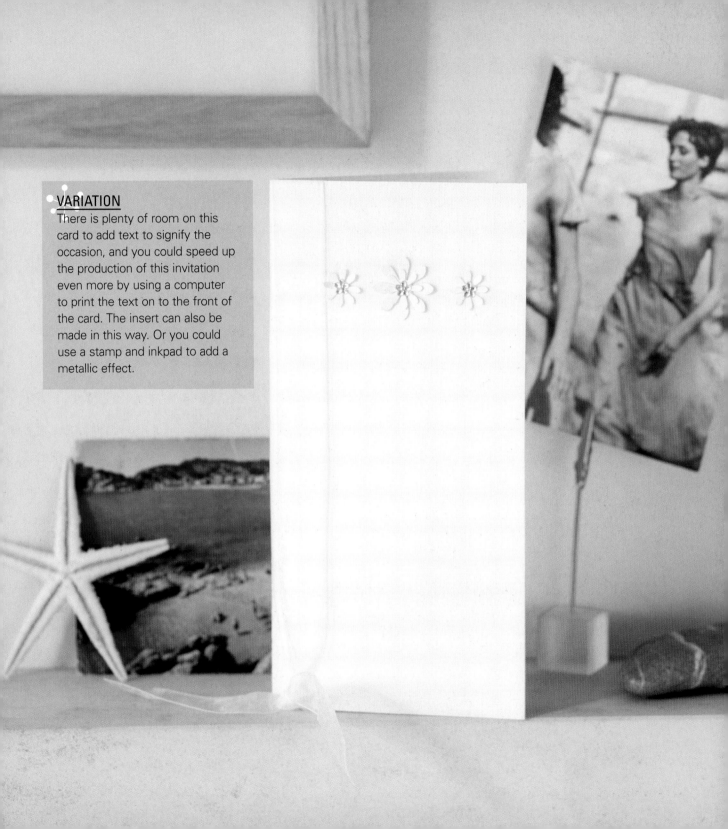

VARIATION

There is plenty of room on this card to add text to signify the occasion, and you could speed up the production of this invitation even more by using a computer to print the text on to the front of the card. The insert can also be made in this way. Or you could use a stamp and inkpad to add a metallic effect.

VARIATION

Sewing onto card is very effective but don't push your sewing machine too far. Use the thinnest card you can and choose a suitable needle. If you'd rather not use a sewing machine, you could handstitch the butterfly trails on or use rub-on transfers that are available in stitch effect. It's such a fast way to make a lovely design that once you've started sewing you could well get the bug!

mother's day

Buttons look beautiful on cards and come in so many different designs. These butterflies are perfect for a gorgeous girlie card to tell your mum how much she means to you.

MATERIALS: Blue glitter skinny card base
Purple pearl card (200mm x 64mm)
Silver thread
3 blue butterfly buttons
1 blue flower button
5mm clear gems

TOOLS: Craft knife, ruler, cutting mat
Sewing machine
Masking tape
Craft glue

STEP 1
On the reverse of the purple card, lightly draw three trails where you want the stitching to go. Using the sewing machine, stitch along these markings with silver thread. You may want to vary the stitch types to add extra interest.

STEP 2
Secure the ends of the thread on the back of the purple card using masking tape. Glue this purple card on to the front of the blue card base so it leaves a border of blue all the way round. Glue a butterfly to the end of each stitched trail, angling them at different directions. Glue the flower in the bottom left corner of the purple card.

STEP 3
Glue the 5mm clear gems over the holes in one of the buttons and add gems to the stitching below the other two butterflies, making each butterfly different.

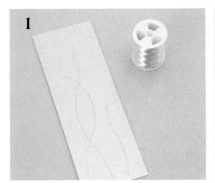

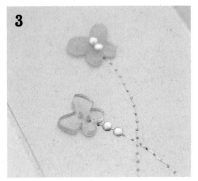

father's day

This striking card has a bold motif to give a more masculine tone. It takes some time to cut out the leaf shapes but it's definitely worth the effort!

MATERIALS: Black tall card base
Extra black card
Gold/brass brads (or paper fasteners)
Gold paper (200 x 95mm)

TOOLS: Scissors
Craft knife and cutting mat
Craft glue

STEP 1

Using the template on the right, trace or draw leaf shapes on to the extra black card. You need six leaves, each one slightly smaller than the previous one. The template is for the smallest size leaf and the biggest one should be twice its size. Cut out the inner segments and lightly score down the spine of each leaf so they can be bent.

STEP 2

Arrange the leaves on the front of the gold paper down the right-hand side. Place the largest one at the top and overlap the others in order of size. Place the last leaf by itself in the bottom right corner. Secure the leaves by gluing down the spine of each leaf.

STEP 3

Add brads on both sides of the leaf layer, on alternate sides. Make a small cut with the knife to push the brads through. Glue the gold paper on to the front of the black card base and lift the edges of the leaves to create a 3D effect.

Leaf template

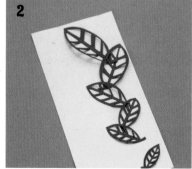

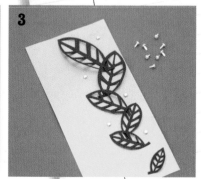

VARIATION
By changing the colours to match the anniversary (such as ruby or diamond), you have a design that can be utilised again and again. Why not try this technique on other shapes of cutout card or trapped in a card with an aperture?

anniversary

This simple yet elegant card is perfect for any anniversary. It can also be used for a wedding acceptance card, a Valentine's card or an invitation to an anniversary celebration. The technique of wrapping thread and adding gems gives the design a delicate finish.

MATERIALS: Ivory A6 card base (unfolded)
Gold paper
Gold card (105 x 148mm)
Ivory card
Gold thread
5mm topaz gems

TOOLS: Glue
Embossing tool and board
Scissors
Masking tape

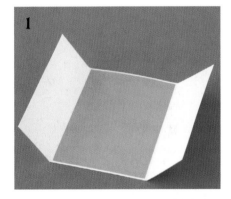

STEP 1
Create a gate-fold base from the ivory card by scoring a line 52mm in from each end. Fold down the lines. Cut the gold paper slightly smaller than the middle section of the card base and glue on to the middle section of the inside of the card.

STEP 2
Using the embossing board, emboss a row of dots along the top and bottom of both front panels.

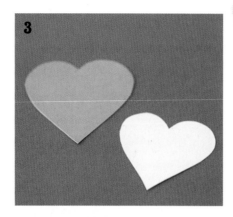

Heart templates

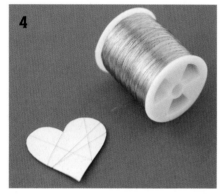

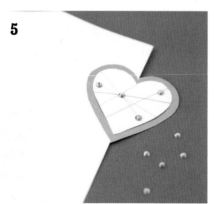

STEP 3
Using the templates above, cut out a large heart in gold card and a smaller heart in ivory card.

STEP 4
Wrap gold thread randomly round the ivory heart. Use masking tape at the back to secure the thread in place.

STEP 5
Glue the ivory heart on the gold heart so there is an equal border round the edge. Turn the heart over and add glue to the right-hand side of the back. Position the heart near the top front of the card, securing it to the left-hand panel only so the card still opens. Glue a few topaz gems on to the thread-wrapped heart, positioning them randomly.

get well

When someone's poorly, a lovingly handmade card can be wonderful medicine. This pretty oriental card is sure to brighten up a bedside.

MATERIALS: Purple pearl large square card base
Oriental paper
Gold wire (24-gauge)
Purple seed beads
Gold star beads

TOOLS: Knife, ruler, cutting mat
Old scissors or wire cutters
Craft glue
Glue gun

For this card you will need to make an origami butterfly from a 40 x 40mm square of gold paper. There are various butterfly designs out there – check out the internet or one of the many origami books available. If you find this too complicated, use a punch or stamp or cutouts to make your butterfly. Butterfly embellishments may also be bought quite easily. It may seem daunting, but once you've tried the origami technique a few times you will probably be able to make it without the instructions. It looks great in all sizes – try a variety of papers (nothing too thick) and you'll soon be hooked!

STEP 1

Use a 40 x 40mm square of gold paper to make an origami butterfly. Try www.youtube.com and searching for origami butterfly – this throws up some good video instructions. There is a variety of other embellishments you could also use – see page 85.

STEP 2

Cut a piece of oriental paper slightly smaller than the front of the card base. Glue in place so there is an equal border of the purple card base showing round the edges.

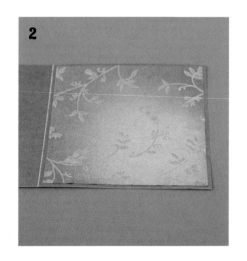

STEP 3

Cut a piece of wire longer than you need (approximately 150mm) and thread a purple bead on. Bend the end of the wire back on itself to stop the bead falling off. Add 9 more beads and then a star. Repeat this twice and end with a row of 10 more purple beads. Try to keep the stars all pointing the same way. Bend the wire at the ends to stop the beads coming off and then trim down the ends.

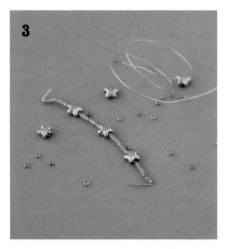

STEP 4

Bend the wire with the beads on it to create a wiggly shape. Apply hot glue from the glue gun to the backs of the stars and secure in position on the card (down the right side). Add a touch of glue to the ends of the wire where it is bent over for added security. Now simply position the butterfly at the top of the wire and glue in place.

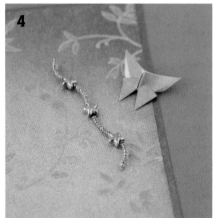

VARIATION

This butterfly card is so unusual that it could inspire you to produce a whole range of cards. Why not use different papers or stiffen some fabric to make it really tactile, even turning it into a badge that you can remove from the card? You could have two or three butterflies, or maybe the butterfly could actually be the card!

new home

Use this technique to create cards for all occasions by changing the colours and the image you emboss. Simple images give the best results; you could use a heart shape or flower, or a snowflake for a wintry card.

MATERIALS: White card (297 x 105mm)
Blue mulberry paper
Silver angel hair paper
Silver sheet metal

TOOLS: Scoring tool
Spray mount and craft glue
Knife, ruler, cutting mat
Thin-tipped permanent marker pen
Embossing tool

STEP 1
Create an A6 card base from the white card by scoring it in half so that the card opens from the bottom instead of the side. Use the spray mount to cover the card base with the mulberry paper, trimming off the excess with the knife and ruler.

Cut a piece of angel hair paper 60 x 50mm and a piece of metal 50 x 40mm.

STEP 2
Practise drawing an image of a house with a sun and a flower on scrap paper. When you are happy with the design, draw it in reverse on the piece of metal using the permanent marker pen.

STEP 3
Place the metal image right side-down on a soft surface such as carpet or foam. Use the embossing tool to go over the drawn lines and produce a raised effect. Turn over to the right side and glue on to the angel hair paper with craft glue. Add more glue to the angel hair paper and position the image on the front of the card base towards the top, in the centre.

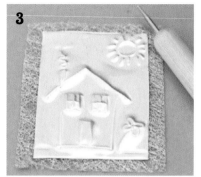

VARIATION
These buttons work really well for a new baby card but why not adapt the idea of using buttons on cards for adults too. There are some really nice novelty buttons on the market which could be used for occasions such as Christmas or Easter, and will add something unusual to your designs.

new baby

Using buttons made for baby clothes is a delightful way to add that newborn feeling to a card. There are so many buttons available that you're sure to find the right colour and animal for a girl, boy, twins or triplets!

MATERIALS: White ribbed skinny card base
2 lengths of blue ribbon in different widths (7mm and 13mm), one decorative and one plain
3 blue elephant buttons
White card
Light blue card

TOOLS: Craft glue
Craft knife, ruler, cutting mat
Glue gun
3D foam squares

STEP 1
Start by laying the widest ribbon down the centre of the front of the card. If the ribbon is long enough, secure it inside the card by gluing the two ends together on the inside so they overlap. If not, trim the ends neatly and glue at the top and bottom of the front of the card. Repeat with the narrower ribbon, laying it down the centre of the wide ribbon.

STEP 2
Cut a piece of white card 60 x 25mm with the ribbed lines running lengthways to match the card base. Cut a piece of blue card 65 x 30mm and glue the white piece on to this.

STEP 3
Using the glue gun, secure the elephant buttons on the mounted white card. Space them equally in a column and hold in place until they are secure. Now attach this piece to the top centre of the card with 3D foam squares so the ribbon runs underneath.

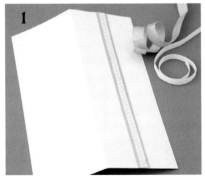

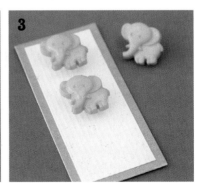

Badge

Corsage

Retro Fabric

Fridge Magnets

Cupcake

something a bit different

The unusual designs in this section will get you thinking really creatively and hopefully inspire your own unique designs. Their quirkiness is sure to bring a smile to whoever receives them!

badge

Badges are really popular again and badge-making kits mean you can create your own unique designs. This contemporary card has a jewelled badge that will add decoration to any bag or jacket.

MATERIALS: White tall card base
Large sheet of paper with a
raised or flock pattern
Clear teardrop gems

TOOLS: Spray mount and craft glue
Knife, ruler, cutting mat
Compass cutter
Badge-maker
Double-sided tape

STEP 1

Stick the textured paper to the card base with spray mount. Trim to size. Decide which size of badge you want to make and use the compass cutter to cut a circle out of the top right corner of the card (lay the card flat so you only cut through the front).

STEP 2

Using the remaining textured paper, find an area that matches the circle you have cut out from the front of the card. Cut out a circle and, following the badge-maker instructions, use this to create a badge (don't add the plastic covering to the badge). If you don't have a badge-maker, make a badge by fixing a badge pin to the back of the circle you cut out from the card.

STEP 3

Position the badge on the card so the pattern lines up and it fits through the hole. Secure the badge on the inside of the card with a piece of double-sided tape, and close the card. Finally, decorate the card and badge with the teardrop gems, incorporating them into the pattern on the paper.

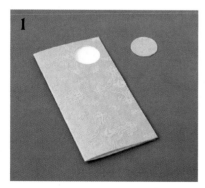

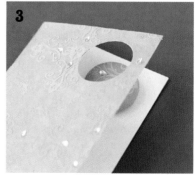

VARIATION

Customise this design to produce badges for all occasions so friends and family can keep the badge as a reminder of the occasion. Paper with a flock effect is making a comeback so investigate what is available to create a really tactile design, or simply use fabric to cover the card so your badges are truly unique. Why limit yourself to one badge per card? Make a row of patterned badges the focal point of a plain coloured card.

corsage card

This card would be ideal as an invitation to a party or a chic hen weekend, but it would work equally as well as a Mother's Day card. The removable corsage means the card is also a gift. Adapt the design depending on the occasion – the recipient can wear the corsage or attach it to a bag or hat to give it an instant makeover.

MATERIALS:

FOR THE CARD
Purple pearl card (210 x 297mm)
0.5 metre of 20mm black
organza ribbon
Plain purple paper (210 x 148mm)
Black vellum or paper (210 x 148mm)

FOR THE CORSAGE
1 metre of 6mm black organza ribbon
1 metre of 3mm black satin ribbon
1 x badge back/pin
1 x 4mm clear gem

TOOLS:

Computer and printer
Craft knife and cutting mat
Scissors
Eyelet tool
Double-sided tape
Craft glue
Spray mount
Metallic pen
Sewing needle and black thread

TO MAKE THE CARD

STEP 1

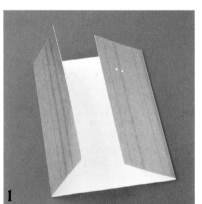

Using a computer, print random purple lines of varying thickness on to the sheet of purple pearl card (the lines should run across the width of the card rather than the height). Score the card across the width 74mm from each end. Fold along these lines to make a gate-fold card.

STEP 2

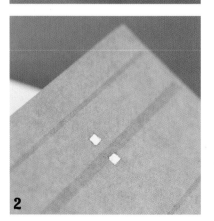

Decide where you want the corsage to be placed and cut two small square holes in the card for the badge pin to go through. Use an eyelet tool to make holes if you prefer. Make the length between these holes shorter than the length of the badge pin, or the card will bend when you attach the pin.

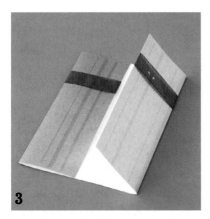

STEP 3

Wrap the 20mm black organza ribbon round the card so it runs from the inside of the front of the card and round the back, finishing on the inside of the card. For neatness make sure the ribbon meets the score lines inside the card. Trim the ends with sharp scissors and use a piece of double-sided tape to secure the ends in place. The tape will prevent the ribbon from fraying. The ribbon should cover the holes you have cut in the card so make sure the ribbon runs over them when you attach it, on the front and inside of the card.

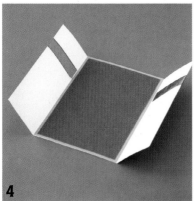

STEP 4

Glue the plain purple paper onto the centre panel inside the card. Trim the black vellum so it is smaller than the purple paper and attach with spray mount, leaving an equal border round the edges. Make the corsage (see overleaf), then attach it to the front of the card through the holes you have made.

Use a metallic purple or silver pen to write your message inside.

VARIATION

This corsage is so straightforward to make that you'll want to make lots, in different sizes, ribbons and colours. Add some old jewellery, such as a chain or some sparkly jewels, so they hang down from the back like your own personalised bag charm.

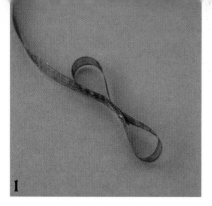

TO MAKE THE CORSAGE

STEP 1

Start with the 6mm black organza ribbon and make a long loop, 40mm long. Secure in place with a dot of glue. Make another loop opposite this and glue in the centre again. The glue may look a bit messy but once the corsage is complete it will be hidden, provided you are careful when applying it!

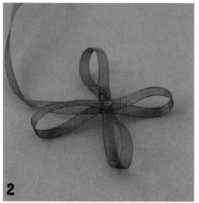

STEP 2

Now make two more loops the same size as the others and glue in place so you have created a sort of X shape. It doesn't matter which side of the corsage you glue the ribbon on as long as you keep it neat.

STEP 3

You need to make eight loops altogether, so keep folding the ribbon back on itself and gluing until you have filled in the remaining gaps with loops. When all eight loops are complete, secure the ribbon in the centre of the corsage with a dot of glue (this will now be the back of the corsage).

STEP 4

Repeat steps 1–3 using the 3mm black satin ribbon to make eight loops in between the organza ones. Try to keep the loops equal in length. When you have finished, glue the ribbon at the back and trim the remainder so a length of it hangs down. Cut another piece of ribbon slightly shorter and glue it to the back of the corsage.

STEP 5

Using the needle and black thread, sew the badge back on to the back of the corsage. If you prefer to use glue, use a glue gun but sewing will give a more secure finish. Finally, glue the clear gem to the centre of the front of the finished corsage.

5

retro fabric

This is a very unusual idea that combines fabric-manipulation techniques with basic card-making skills to give a visually exciting and tactile design!

MATERIALS: 2 white tall card bases
Bold patterned fabric
(preferably lightweight)

TOOLS: Fabric scissors (or sharp scissors)
Double-sided tape
Iron
Craft knife, ruler, cutting mat
Craft glue

STEP 1

Lay one card base on the fabric and cut around the edges,
allowing enough extra fabric to create folds from. Cut the fabric
so it is 20mm larger than the card base on the top, bottom and
right-hand side. Make the allowance on the left-hand side the same
size as the whole card base.

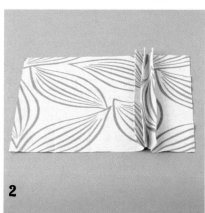

STEP 2

Put the card base aside and gather the material to form three
concertina-like folds, positioned closely together. Make sure the
folds are not too close to the edge of the fabric, otherwise you
may lose some of the design when you fold the edges of the fabric
around the card. When you are happy with the size and spacing of
the folds, cut three strips of double-sided tape and, working on the
wrong side of the fabric, place a piece of tape inside each fold, then
press the fold together.

STEP 3

Set the iron at the right temperature for your fabric. When ready, use it to sharpen the folds in the fabric, flattening them down on to the card. Hold down the centre section of the folds with one hand and use the iron to press the folds on either side of your hand in the opposite direction. Be careful with your fingers at this point! When you let go, you should have created a twist in the fabric. Manipulate the folds until you're happy with this twist.

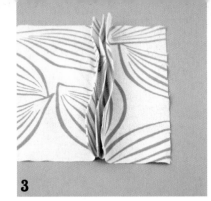

STEP 4

Lay the fabric right side down and lay the card base on top. Position the card so you have an equal border all the way round, cutting the longer edge so it matches the other sides. The folds you have made will be too bulky to fold round the card so trim the ends of the folds that overlap the edges.

STEP 5

Apply double-sided tape round the edges of the front of the card, including the spine. Add tape inside the card round the outside edges only. Stick the card base on to the fabric and smooth out any air pockets. Fold the edges round into the inside and secure in place over the tape.

STEP 6

Trim the second white card base slightly smaller than the first and add glue down all the edges including the spine. Secure it in place inside the card so only a slight edge of the fabric is revealed.

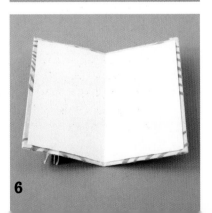

VARIATION

This card looks so impressive but the technique is really easy to master. Experiment with various fabrics and if you're feeling bold use different sewing techniques to create other 3D effects.

cupcake

This card is a gift and a greeting all in one, as the 'pocket' in the front holds a recipe for making yummy cupcakes. It is great as a birthday card or party invitation, and the best part is that you get to eat the cupcakes once you've photographed them! So put your oven gloves on and get baking, or if you don't trust your icing skills, take a photo of some in your local bakery. If you do that, you can skip Step 1.

STEP 1

Follow the recipe on the right, or use your own cupcake recipe.

When you are happy with the presentation, take a photo of your best cupcake with a digital camera.

LEMON AND CHOCOLATE CUPCAKES
Makes 8–10 cupcakes

INGREDIENTS

8–10 cupcake cases
115g soft butter
115g caster sugar
115g self-raising flour
50g plain flour
2 large eggs, whisked

Grated rind and juice of 1 lemon
50g good-quality white or milk
chocolate, broken into small pieces
115g icing sugar
Coloured sprinkles and cake candles
(or other preferred decoration)

Preheat the oven to 160°C/325°F/gas mark 3 and arrange the cupcake cases on a bun tray.

Place the butter, sugar, flour, eggs and lemon rind in a large bowl and mix everything together well. Stir the chocolate in so it is evenly distributed through the mixture and then fill each case about three-quarters full.

Cook on the middle shelf of the oven for approximately 25 minutes until golden. Remove from the oven and allow the cakes to cool in the tray for 5 minutes.

Put the icing sugar in a bowl and add splashes of lemon juice, stirring until it is a thick spreading consistency.

Spread the icing on top of the cakes and decorate with coloured sprinkles or other decoration of your choice. Add a candle to each cake if desired.

MATERIALS: Brown card (297 x 420 mm)
Felt-tip pens (optional)
White card
Red card (50 x 45mm)
150mm thin red ribbon
Gold star confetti

TOOLS: Craft knife, ruler, cutting mat
Computer and printer
Craft glue
Eyelet, eyelet tool and
hammer (or use a holepunch)

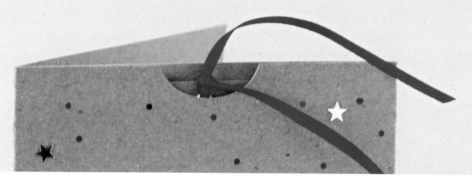

STEP 2

Cut the brown card so it measures 210 x 315mm and keep the
leftover in reserve. Score twice to create three equal sections
measuring 210 x 105mm each but do not fold yet. Using a
computer, print multi-coloured dots on the centre panel or
alternatively use felt-tip pens to make the dots. Fold down the score
lines so the panels lie flat behind the central, polka-dotted section.

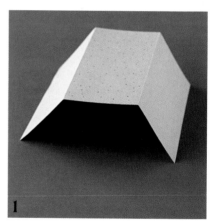

STEP 3

Print out the photo of the cupcake on the white card so it measures
45 x 40mm. Cut it out and mount it in the centre of the red card.

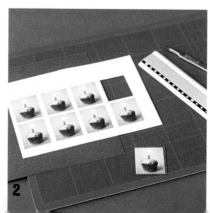

STEP 4

Type out your recipe in a fancy font, leaving enough space between the title and ingredients to glue in the photo (you can write it out by hand if you prefer). Leave a gap at the top of the page so you can add an eyelet later. Print the recipe out on the reserved brown card and trim down to 190 x 80mm (it has to be smaller than the card sections so it will fit inside the pocket).

STEP 5

Lay the card base out flat. Cut a 50 x 45mm window in the polka-dotted centre panel, using the printed recipe as a guide to where it should be positioned. This is where the cupcake picture on the recipe card is going to show through so it is important that the square is cut out in the right place – don't make the incision until you are sure! Draw a semi-circle in pencil at the top of the centre panel and cut away with the knife, rubbing out any pencil marks that still show.

STEP 6

Turn the card base over so you are working on the inside. Line the bottom and left edge with glue, then fold this left-hand panel in so it lies flat behind the centre panel, creating a pocket. Leave to dry.

STEP 7

Using the eyelet tool and hammer, add an eyelet to the top of the recipe card, tying a short piece of ribbon through the hole. (If you don't have an eyelet tool, you can use a hole punch and just thread ribbon through the hole instead.) Finally, glue a star to each corner of the recipe and in random positions on the front until you are happy with the design.

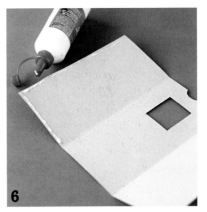

VARIATION

You could personalise the card even more by icing a message on the cake before you photograph it. You can substitute the cupcake with your own favourite recipe, or adapt the pocket idea to include a favourite poem or personalised message. Alternatively, you could send out the cupcakes as your party invitations, icing each cake with the name of a guest and putting it in a little cake box. Make smaller versions of the card with party details printed on the back, and attach to the cake boxes with ribbon.

fridge magnets

Glam up your friend's kitchen by giving her this fabulous birthday card! A girl can never have too many handbags, and these will make her smile whenever she goes to the fridge!

MATERIALS: Bright pink tall card base
Wrapping paper with handbags
or other accessories design
Circular magnet backs
Silver cord and mini pegs
Small white stickers
Masking tape

TOOLS: Craft knife, cutting mat
Scissors
Laminator
Glue gun
Eyelet tool and hammer

STEP 1

Select the images you want to use and carefully cut them out.
Cut out the space inside the bag handles. Follow the laminator
instructions and laminate the handbags.

STEP 2

Cut out the handbags leaving a border of plastic so the design doesn't come apart. Cut out the space inside the bag handles. Turn over the handbags and using the glue gun, attach a circular magnet to the back of each.

STEP 3

Turn the card landscape and, using the eyelet tool, make a hole at either end of the card about 2cm down from the top. Cut a length of silver cord long enough to hang down between the holes. Tie a knot near each end; thread the ends of the cord through the holes so the knots cover the holes on the front of the card. Secure the loose ends on the reverse of the card with small white stickers.

STEP 4

Decide how you want the handbags to be positioned. Using small pieces of masking tape, secure the magnets to the card. Now add the pegs.
This card is quite fragile and would be best given in a box; likewise the magnetic element may mean the card shouldn't be posted.

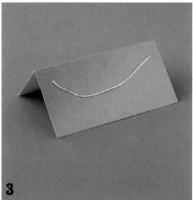

VARIATION

These laminated handbags are made from wrapping paper with magnets attached to the back but you could create your own by using images from magazines or catalogues. How about different items of clothing to make it look like a real washing line, or maybe just a row of brightly coloured knickers!

Computer

Punches

Sewing

Spray Painting

gallery

This section covers four techniques: punches, sewing, spray painting and using a computer. There are ideas for adapting each technique so you can get the most out of your equipment.

BLUE FLOWER

This simple image is a close-up of the centre of a flower. The unusual view gives the image quite an abstract, contemporary feel. Use your software to adjust the colour balance on your photos, creating unexpected results! Interest is also added here by printing some of the petal shapes on to vellum, cutting them out and gluing them on top of the card to produce a 3D effect.

WARHOL

People always make interesting subjects for photographs. Personalise a card for someone's birthday by using a photo of them. Here I've given my friend Brigid the Andy Warhol treatment! This is a simple repeat using the same photo in different colours. It would work well for numerous subjects, including family pets!

computer

Using a computer to create designs will open up a whole new world of options. The designs shown here should give you some ideas on how to turn your home photography and other imagery into stunning cards.

LEAF REPEAT

Don't just stick to a full photo for the front of the card. Reducing the image and repeating it to create a pattern produces a new image altogether. This is a fantastic way to make your own background papers (and wrapping paper, too) as you can make the repeat as subtle or as complicated as you choose.

TREE

Vary the types of papers you print your photos on and you may be surprised by how much an image can change. Here I've used vellum, which gives the image a soft finish, while the black card behind helps emphasise the pastel shades in the sky. Let yourself think outside the box: turn your photos into mini works of art by creating shapes or structures so they aren't always flat. Or make a collage by tearing the image into pieces and then reassembling it in a different way.

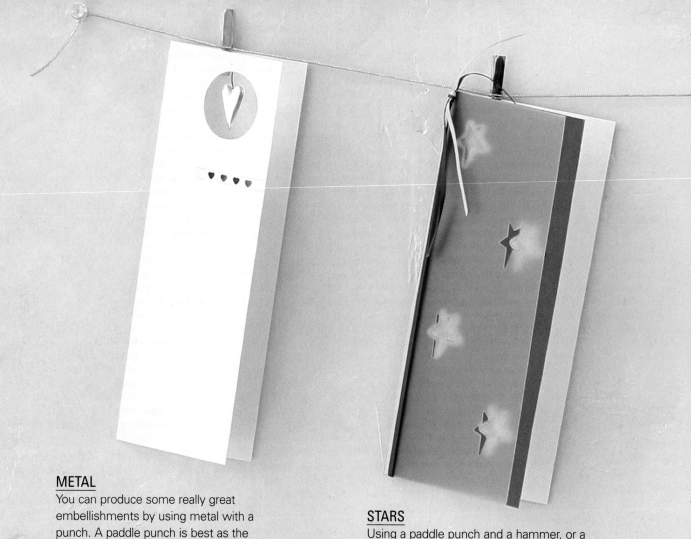

METAL

You can produce some really great embellishments by using metal with a punch. A paddle punch is best as the force of the hammer helps punch through the metal, but some smaller punches will do the job, too.

STARS

Using a paddle punch and a hammer, or a lever punch with a long handle, gives you the freedom to punch a shape anywhere in your card. Using a hammer means you can apply more force so you can create designs with tougher materials such as polypropylene.

punches

Punches are a staple of the card-maker's toolbox and they open the door to numerous designs. You can buy all sorts of punches, which means you can experiment with a variety of techniques and materials.

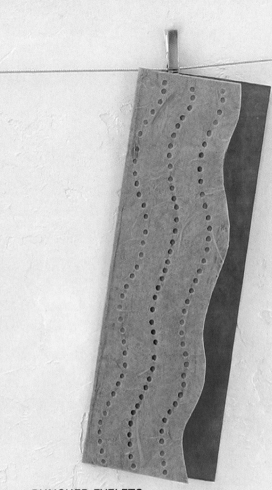

PUNCHED EYELETS

Another use for the eyelet tool is to create patterns and shapes by punching out holes. Add interest by changing the end of the tool to make holes of varying sizes. Lay a piece of bright or patterned paper underneath the punched paper and the colour will show through. You could use this technique to spell out a message or a number on a birthday card.

FABRIC

This card uses a punch to create a repeat pattern out of material. Die-cutting tools designed for crafters are available and are worth investing in if you plan on card making being a lifetime hobby! They cut through heavier materials such as fabric, light plastic and thin metal sheeting, as well as layers of paper at a time, saving you time and effort. Many craft shops will die-cut shapes for you, and lots of other templates and die-cut shapes can be bought on the internet.

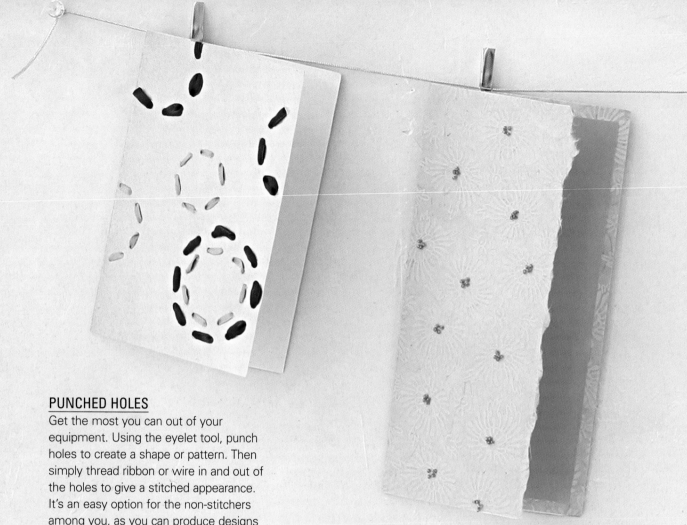

PUNCHED HOLES

Get the most you can out of your equipment. Using the eyelet tool, punch holes to create a shape or pattern. Then simply thread ribbon or wire in and out of the holes to give a stitched appearance. It's an easy option for the non-stitchers among you, as you can produce designs as simple or complicated as you wish.

BEADS

Sewing beads on this handmade paper gives the card a delicate appearance. If patience is not your virtue, just stitch a few beads on to a central motif or mounted emblem, keeping the work to a minimum. Or simply add one or two beads in various places to embellish the existing pattern.

sewing

There are many ways to produce a stitching effect – you don't need to be a super stitcher or even own a sewing machine. Stitching is now seen often in shop-bought handmade cards and gives a modern twist to an old-fashioned skill.

BUTTONS

Using the sewing machine without any thread can produce designs really quickly. Don't keep to the same stitch or sewing in straight lines – take risks and see where the machine takes you! Add embellishments to the finished design such as buttons (sewn or glued on), beads, gems or eyelets.

SNOWFLAKE SHAPE

Handsewing without any thread leaves a more distinct outline. Use a sharp, strong needle, pricking tool or other sharp point to push though the card. Create your own shapes or outline round existing patterns. Backing the card with a darker colour inside will make the dots stand out even more.

BLUE WITH PINK STARS
Spray paint is used here to cover most of the card. Why limit yourself to only decorating the outside of a card, when there are so many ways to liven up the inside, too?

BLACK AND GOLD
This is an alternative to the festive card on page 59, which shows how a few simple adjustments to the card base and stencil can result in a card suitable for a completely different occasion. I've used shaped ribbons, which give fantastic outlines when sprayed, but anything with a strong silhouette will work well.

spray painting

Spray painting isn't solely for graffiti artists – I love it because it's quick and easy and gives very effective results. Remember to follow the manufacturer's advice when using spray paint.

FLOWERS

This design is based on the idea of revealing areas of the paper underneath. By using patterned or multi-coloured paper for the card base, you can create unusual images that look more difficult than they actually are. This card base was simply covered in wrapping paper before punched shapes were applied to protect areas of the pattern. Try using a combination of papers and spray paints to achieve a really striking effect.

LAYERED PAPERS

Spray painting doesn't have to be the main focus of a card – it can also be used to make your own background papers. Here I have used three different colours sprayed on to gold card. Angel hair paper was laid on top before spraying and has left a delicate outline behind. Experiment with various colours and papers or other materials that have an open weave suitable for creating an outline. Making your own papers adds another element to your cards and can become as simple or involved as you like.

useful addresses

English Stamp
Ships outside UK
(will create personalised
rubber stamps from images
or drawings)
Worth Matravers
Dorset
BH19 3JP
Tel: (01929) 439 1117
www.englishstamp.com

Get Creative
100 Portobello High Street,
Edinburgh
EH15 1AL
Tel: (0131) 669 5214
www.getcreativeonline.co.uk

Helios Fountain
7 Grassmarket
Edinburgh
EH1 2HY
Tel: (0131) 229 7884
www.helios-fountain.co.uk

Heritage Rubber Stamps
c/o Stampers Grove
92 Grove Street, Edinburgh
EH3 8AP
Tel: (0131) 221 9440
www.heritagerubberstamps.com

John Lewis Plc
Branches throughout
the UK (check online for your
nearest store)
Flagship store:
John Lewis Plc
Oxford Street
London
W1A 1EX
Tel: (0207) 629 7711
www.johnlewis.com

Lakeland
Supplies card bases, card punches,
stickers and lots more.
www.lakeland.co.uk

The Mulberry Bush
Shipping worldwide
Limberlost Farm
Swife Lane
Broad Oak
East Sussex
TN21 8UX
Tel: (01435) 882 014
www.themulberry-bush.com

Nineteen Seventy Three
Collection of inspirational wrapping
paper, cards and accessories. Buy online
or check for your nearest stockist
Tel: (01273) 241 294
www.nineteenseventythree.com

Paper Cellar
UK and US versions of the website
available as well as shipping to both
Langley Place
99 Langley Road
Watford
Hertfordshire
WD17 4AU
Tel: (08718) 713 711
www.papercellar.com

Paper Cellar LLC
550 Kane Court
Suite 100
Oviedo
FL 32675
Tel: (+1) 800 805 0818

Paperchase
Various branches throughout the UK;
check online for your nearest store
www.paperchase.co.uk

Items cannot be purchased from this
website; some items are available
through www.amazon.co.uk or call
(0161) 839 1500
Flagship store:
213–215 Tottenham Court Road,
London
W1T 7PS
Tel: (0207) 467 6200
Paperchase has concessions in Borders
bookshops throughout the USA as well
as selected stores in Australia, Dublin
and Singapore.

The Paper People
Producers of fine quality card stock and
decorative papers for card making
25 Hardengreen Industrial Estate
Dalkeith
EH22 3NX
Tel: (0131) 654 4300
www.southfield–stationers.co.uk

Roger La Bourde
Range of contemporary stationery.
Check online for your nearest stockist
87 Kingsgate Road,
London
NW6 4JY
Tel: (0207) 328 0491
www.rogerlabourde.com

1407 11th Avenue
Seattle
WA 98122
Tel: (+1) 877 623 7275

Dederingstr. 10 d-12107,
Berlin
Germany
Tel: (030) 69 58 23 60

acknowledgements

Having the luck to work on this book has been a fantastic experience and most definitely worth all the hard work! I'm so pleased with the finished book and the way it has come together, and it's all down to the efforts of many dedicated people. In particular I would like to say a special thanks to my editor Jenny Wheatley and my photographer Charlie Richards, both of whom made long days in the studio and all that travelling worth the effort! Thank you both for making this book a pleasure to work on.

I am also extremely grateful to all at Kyle Cathie who made this book possible. I would particularly like to thank Muna Reyal for giving me the opportunity to work on this project. Many thanks also to Shelley Doyle, the book designer, and Lise Manavit, Roberta Pitrè, Tom Richards, Avril Murphy, Rachael Mossom and Heather Pennell who did a great job modelling with the cards! I would also like to mention my thanks to my friend Rachel Henderson for suggesting that I would be the right person for this project.

I would also like to thank to following people for their continued support and encouragement throughout the completion of this book: my family, especially my mum and dad, my good friends Kirsty, Brigid and Karolyne, as well as Lorna Stenhouse (probably the best line manager in the world!).

Finally I'd like to thank all my colleagues at John Lewis Edinburgh who have taken an interest in this project, and Adele and Liz, my former colleagues at 'Finishing touches by Adele', who gave me the opportunity to make cards all day long!

index